AF428738

This book
belongs to:

____

____

____

____

Copyright© 2023. All rights reserved.

No part of this publication may be reproduced, distributed, or transmitted in any form or by any means, including photocopying, recording, or other electronic or mechanical methods, without the prior written permission of the publisher, except in the case of brief quotations embodied in critical reviews and certain other non-commercial uses permitted by copyright law.

First published 2023 with an exclusive licence from the authors to CHEETAH® Purrrrrrr Publishing, an imprint of CHEETAH® Toys & More, LLC (CHEETAH®).

Contact us: 1-860-781-1276, 1-876-909-6311 (WhatsApp), info@mycheetahacademy.com; paulettetrowers@yahoo.com

ISBN-13: 979-8-3303-5064-3
ISBN-10: 8-3303-5064-3

Dear CHEETAH® family:

Our little books were specially created to help our early readers master their decoding skills and build reading fluency. The repetitive use of high-frequency words, word families, decodable words, rhymes, and vivid illustrations facilitates this process. Our stories complement the objectives and content highlighted in the Jamaica Early Childhood Curriculum Guide and the Ministry of Education and Youth Grade I National Standards Curriculum.

In journeying through our series, our little ones will develop a deeper awareness of and appreciation for our Jamaican culture. Our books also have universal appeal, as any early reader can identify with the characters, events and subjects in our texts. Readers will get to enjoy the stories, build vocabulary, and exercise critical thinking by engaging in the activities at the end of each story.

Additionally, as a precursor to our series, or as a support to it, we've created a decodable 'sentence strip' book for the very young readers and those who require more scaffolding.

Happy reading!

CHEETAH®

Chasing and capturing your dreams with you.

C-DER™
CHEETAH Decodable & Early Readers
Learning the alphabet is like going on a treasure hunt to find hidden words. Let's go! Let's go on a treasure hunt for words!

My decodable words:

nap, tap, Ben, hen, pen, get,
let, big, pig, sip, tip, got,
hot, lot, not, spot, fuss, Gus

Letter sound:

- hard consonant sound /g/ in the initial, medial and final positions in words

Word families: 'ap', 'en', 'et', 'ig', 'ip', 'ot', 'us'

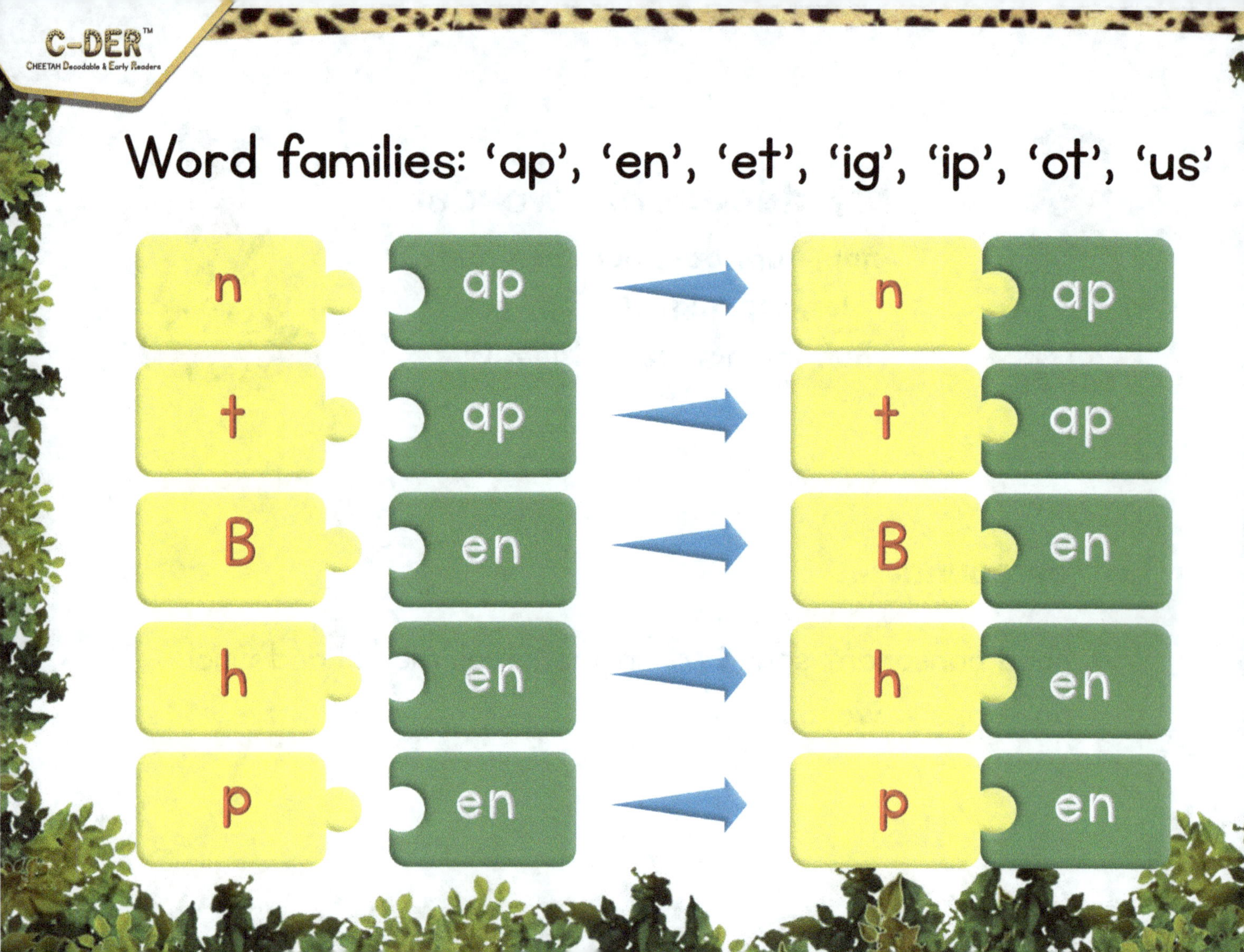

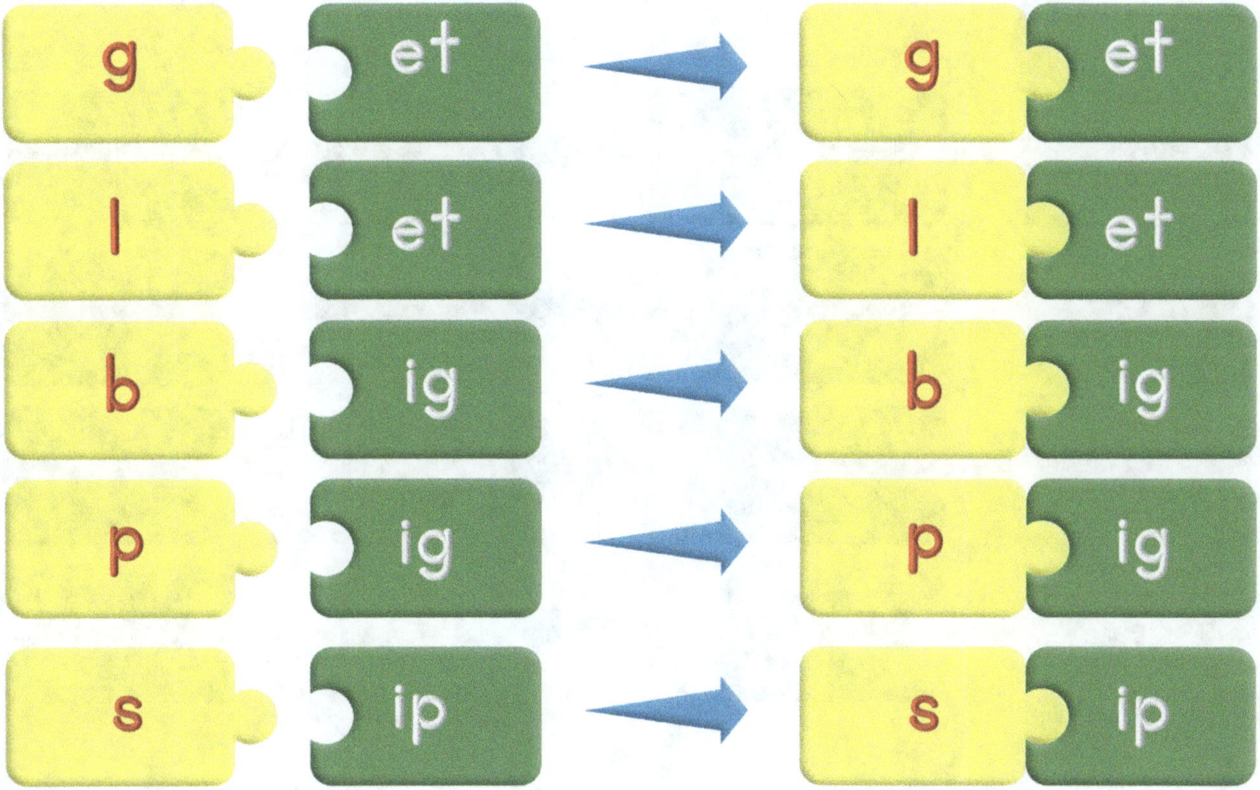

g	et	→	g et
l	et	→	l et
b	ig	→	b ig
p	ig	→	p ig
s	ip	→	s ip

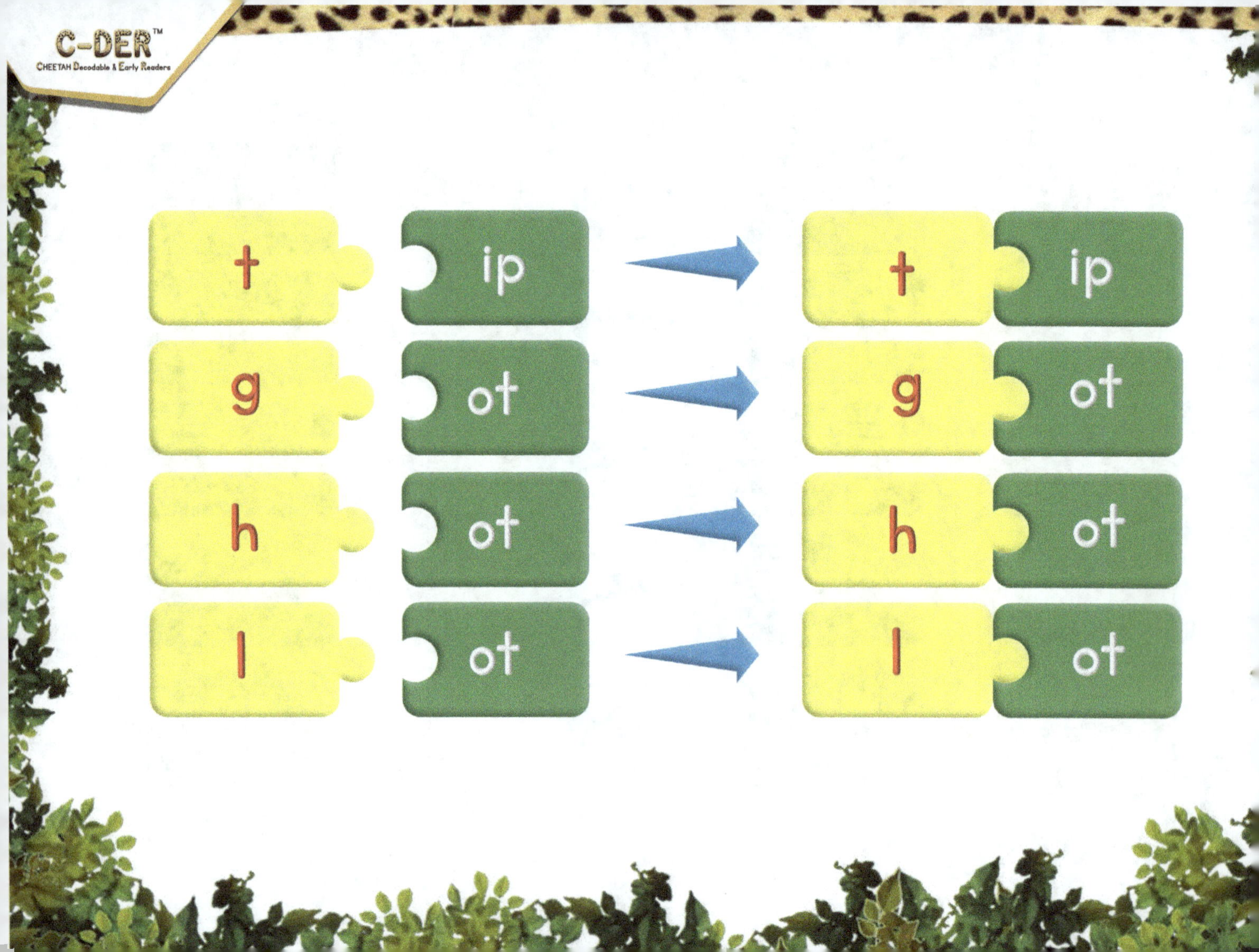

C-DER™
CHEETAH Decodable & Early Readers
t ip
g ot
h ot
l ot
t ip
g ot
h ot
l ot

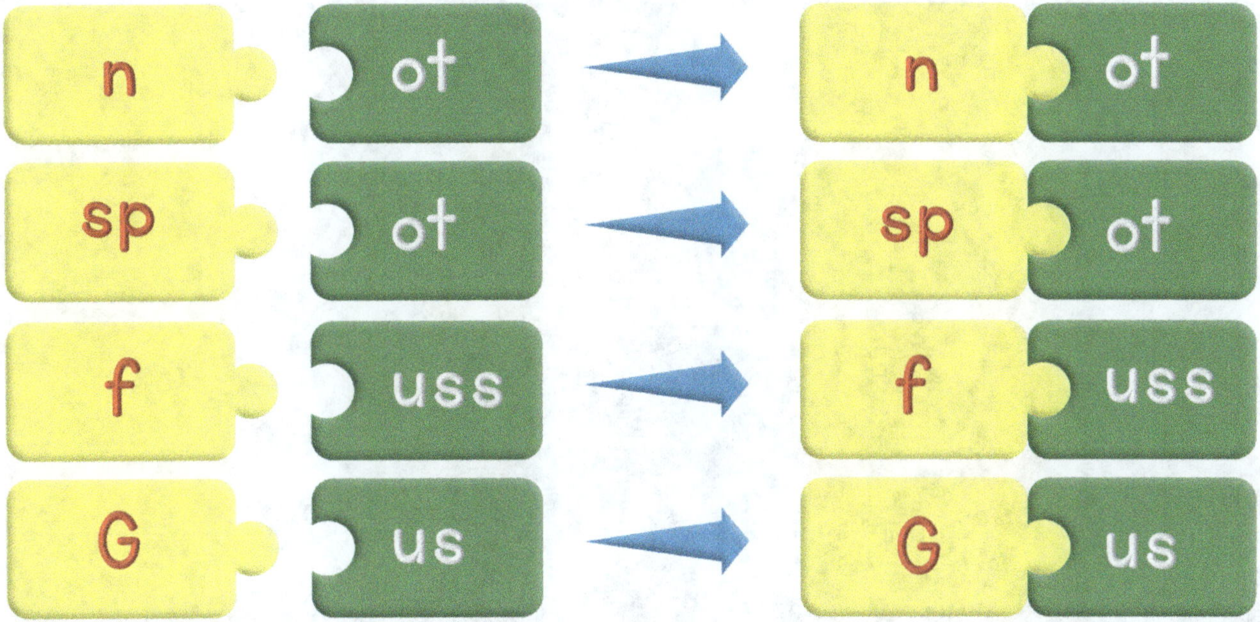

n	ot	→	n	ot
sp	ot	→	sp	ot
f	uss	→	f	uss
G	us	→	G	us

1

Glenda Needs Help

'I got a new goat. Do you want to see her?

She is a brown goat. We call her Glenda.'

'Yes,' says Gus. 'Is she very big?

Is she as big as your dog or as big as a pig?'

C-DER
CHEETAH Decodable & Early Readers
3

'Let us go out to see her now,' says Ben.

'She is out in the yard. She is in a pen.'

They go out in the yard and walk to the pen.

As they pass, they say 'hi' to Hilda the hen.

5

They stop by the pen of Glenda the goat.

She looks very pretty in her brown coat.

'I think she needs some water,' Ben says.

'She drinks a lot of water on very hot days.'

'Let us go to get her water from the tap.

Let us go now before she takes her nap.'

They fill the little pail to the tip.

They get a lot of water for Glenda to sip.

9

When they get near the pen, Gus says, 'Look at the goat!

What is that thing that sits on her coat?'

Ben says, 'It looks like a bug or a bee.'

Gus says, 'It looks more like a bee to me.'

C-DER
CHEETAH Decodable & Early Readers
11

Then Glenda the goat starts to make a fuss.

'Look! See the bee fly away,' says Gus.

Glenda is not happy. Did the bee sting her?

She jumps about.... Oops! Glenda falls over!

Glenda starts to bleat and bleat.

She cannot get back on her feet!

The boys go in the pen to help her.

Now is a good time to give her the water.

14

C-DER
CHEETAH Decodable & Early Readers
15

Glenda drinks the water then sits on the grass.

Glenda looks out for the bee, alas....

The boys rub the spot on her coat where it stung her.

Ben says, 'It's okay. The bee won't come back, Glenda.'

Discussion and activities:

1. Have the children talk about a time when they had to help their pet or some other animal.

2. Have the children identify the words with the target letter and sound.

3. Have the children make the sound of the target letter and identify rhyming words in the text.

Discussion and activities:

4. Discuss the words *bleat* and *oops* as used in the context of the story.

5. Have the children read the text aloud.

18

Questions:

1. What do you think the author means by 'in her brown coat'?

   ....

2. Why did Glenda start to bleat?

   ....

www.ingramcontent.com/pod-product-compliance
Lightning Source LLC
Chambersburg PA
CBHW081205130726
47996CB00009B/3250